Thomas Edison

by Lucia Raatma

Compass Point Early Biographies

Content Adviser: Robert K. L. Wheeler,
President, Edison Birthplace Association,
Milan, Ohio

Reading Adviser: Dr. Linda D. Labbo,
Department of Reading Education, College of Education,
The University of Georgia

COMPASS POINT BOOKS
Minneapolis, Minnesota

Compass Point Books
3109 West 50th Street, #115
Minneapolis, MN 55410

Visit Compass Point Books on the Internet at *www.compasspointbooks.com*
or e-mail your request to *custserv@compasspointbooks.com*

Editor: Christianne C. Jones
Photo Researcher: Marcie C. Spence
Designer/Page Production: Bradfordesign, Inc./Les Tranby

Library of Congress Cataloging-in-Publication Data
Raatma, Lucia.
　　Thomas Edison / by Lucia Raatma.
　　　　p. cm.—(Compass Point early biographies)
Summary: Simple text describes the life and accomplishments of Thomas Alva Edison,
inventor of the phonograph, electric lightbulb, and many other devices.
Includes bibliographical references and index.
ISBN 0-7565-0567-4 (hardcover)
1. Edison, Thomas A. (Thomas Alva), 1847-1931—Juvenile literature. 2. Inventors—
United States—Biography—Juvenile literature. 3. Electric engineers—United States—
Biography—Juvenile literature. [1. Edison, Thomas A. (Thomas Alva), 1847-1931. 2. Inventors.]
I. Title. II. Series.
　　TK140.E3R33 2004
　　621.3'092–dc22　　　　　　　　　　　　　　　　　　　　　　2003012282

Table of Contents

NOTE: In this book, words that are defined in the glossary
*are in **bold** the first time they appear in the text*

Bright Ideas

Did you turn on a light today? Did you listen to a CD? If you did either one, you can thank Thomas Edison!

Thomas Edison was a talented inventor. He had a lot of great ideas. Edison is known for inventing the lightbulb. He also invented the phonograph, a machine that plays and records sounds. Without the phonograph, we probably would not have CDs and DVDs. Thomas Edison's bright ideas led to many inventions that are still used today.

◄ Thomas Edison invented the electric lightbulb, the phonograph, and many other important devices.

Young Businessman

Thomas Alva Edison was the youngest of seven children. He was born in Milan, Ohio, on February 11, 1847. The Edison family moved to Port Huron, Michigan, when Thomas was 7 years old.

Samuel Edison

Nancy Elliott Edison

Thomas only went to school for about three months. His mother, Nancy Elliott, taught him from home. She had been a teacher earlier in her life. Thomas enjoyed reading and doing experiments. His father, Samuel Edison, was a businessman. Thomas learned many business techniques from him.

◀ Edison's birthplace in Milan, Ohio

Thomas was eager to try
new things. He built models
of engines and mills. He
grew vegetables on the
family farm and sold them
at markets. When Thomas
was 12 years old, he became
a successful businessman. He
sold newspapers, sandwiches,

Edison loved to learn and always
wanted to try new things.

and candy on trains between Detroit and
Port Huron. This business did so well that he
soon hired other people to work for him. By
the time he was 15, Thomas was publishing
his own newspaper.

Learning About the Telegraph

Edison at age 14

While still a teenager, Thomas became a hero. He rescued a young boy from the path of an oncoming railroad car. The boy's father was a **telegraph** operator and was very grateful to Thomas.

In return for Thomas's brave act, he showed Thomas how to use a telegraph. The telegraph used Morse code to send messages. Morse code is a series of dots and dashes that stand for letters and words.

General operating department of Western Union Telegraph Company around 1875

Thomas used his knowledge of the telegraph to find a job. Thomas was 16 when he began working as a telegraph operator for the Western Union Telegraph Company.

By this time in his life, Thomas had developed hearing problems. However, he was still able to understand messages that people were sending to one another.

Becoming an Inventor

When Thomas Edison was 21, he moved to Boston. He continued to work as a telegraph operator. He helped

Edison invented this new version of the stock ticker.

improve the city's fire alarm system and began working on his own inventions.

In 1868, Edison applied for his first **patent** for the electric vote recorder. The next year, he moved to New York City. While in New York, Edison helped make **stock tickers** work better.

11

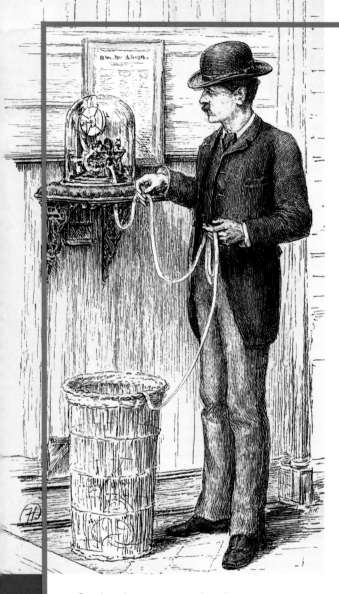

Stock tickers were used in the New York Stock Exchange.

In 1870, Edison moved to Newark, New Jersey. He started a company that made stock tickers, and he continued to work on other inventions.

The quadruplex was one invention he was working on. It was a telegraph that could send four messages at once.

A Family Man

Thomas Edison
believed in hard work,
but he tried to make
time for a family, too.
Mary Stillwell was a
young woman who
worked in Edison's lab.

Mary Stillwell Edison, 1871

The two fell in love and were married on
Christmas Day of 1871. Thomas and Mary had
three children together—Marion Estelle,
Thomas Alva Jr., and William Leslie. Edison
called his first two children Dot and Dash as
a reminder of his work with the telegraph.

13

Working at Menlo Park

Thomas Edison around 1880

In 1876, Edison built a new laboratory in Menlo Park. This area was about 25 miles outside Newark. In his new lab, Edison worked on improving the telephone. The telephone was known as the speaking telegraph at that time. Edison created a **transmitter** that made the telephone work better. People could hear one another more clearly with Edison's transmitter.

Today, we often use machines like phone answering machines and VCRs to record and play back sounds. In the late 1800s, recording sound was a new idea. Edison was one of the first people to work on ways to record sound.

Advertisement for Edison's phonographs

Edison wanted to find a way for telephone and telegraph messages to be recorded and played back. While working on such an invention, he created the phonograph in 1877.

Before long, people came up with the idea of playing music on the phonograph. Edison was now recognized as an important scientist. People called him the "Wizard of Menlo Park."

Edison stands next to one of his first phonographs.

Electricity and the Lightbulb

Not many homes or businesses had electricity in the 1880s. Most people relied on candles and lanterns for light. Edison thought electric lighting was possible. He studied the work of other scientists. He went to meetings where they explained their inventions.

Edison and his team work on a new type of lamp in his Menlo Park lab in 1879.

Edison designed his lightbulb after the 1875 patent he bought from inventors Henry Woodward and Matthew Evans. In 1879, Edison introduced his version of the electric lightbulb.

Because electricity was not common, few people could use the lightbulb. Edison wanted to make electricity more available.

In 1881, he moved back to New York City. He worked on building the Pearl Street Station, a steam electric **power plant.** It opened in 1882. Edison worked on getting

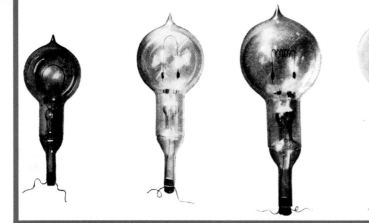

Edison's early version of the electric lightbulb is second from the right. It is shown with three other versions of the early lightbulb.

Men working in Edison's first power plant, Pearl Street Station

power plants built throughout the country. He wanted everyone to have electricity.

Edison joined a group of people to create other electric equipment like power cables, lighting **fixtures,** and **generators.** In 1892, the Edison Electric Light Company and the Thomson-Houston Electric Company formed the General Electric Company.

A Second Marriage

In 1884, Mary Edison died. Thomas Edison continued his work and did his best to raise their three children.

Mina Miller Edison

In 1885, Edison met a young woman named Mina Miller. They married the next year. Together, they had three children—Madeleine, Charles, and Theodore.

Edison wasn't able to spend much time with his family because of his dedication to his work. ➤

Thomas Edison spent many long hours in his laboratory. He often worked 18 hours a day! While Thomas was working, Mina took care of their family and their home. She busied herself with their children and **charity** work.

Edison spent a lot of time in his West Orange lab. It was his second home.

A Bigger Laboratory

Thomas Edison had done amazing things in his Menlo Park laboratory. However, Edison decided to build a larger laboratory in West Orange, New Jersey. In fact, it was 10 times larger than the one in Menlo Park! Inside the new building, Edison had an office filled with books. He also had space to perform experiments and manufacture products.

Edison's Black Maria movie studio was built in 1893. ➤

← peephole

The first kinetoscopes showed films that lasted about one minute.

One invention from the West Orange lab was the kinetoscope. This machine marked a beginning for motion pictures. A person looked through a peephole on a kinetoscope to watch a short movie. Edison soon began working with others to produce motion pictures. His movie studio was called the Black Maria.

Edison and his "Insomnia Squad" take a break to eat. The Insomnia Squad often worked on new inventions straight through the night.

From his lab in West Orange, Edison continued to work on new ideas. He created new ways to process iron ore. He produced a new type of cement. He made batteries that were lighter and easier to use. Edison invented the mimeograph, which eventually led to today's copy machines. He also experimented with different ways of making rubber. Edison held patents on more than 1,000 inventions!

24

Thomas Edison working in his lab in the late 1920s ➤

A Life That Changed the World

Throughout his life, Thomas Edison always believed in hard work. He liked good ideas. He knew long hours were important for those ideas

to become practical inventions. He once said, "Opportunity is missed by most people because it is dressed in overalls and looks like work."

Thomas Edison had a number of illnesses toward the end of his life. Even though he was nearly deaf, Edison continued to work until the very end. He died at his home in Llewellyn Park, New Jersey, on October 18, 1931. He was 84 years old.

His funeral was on October 21. Later that evening, lights at the White House and throughout the country were dimmed for one minute. This short period of darkness honored the man who had brought light and bright ideas to the world.

Edison lived in Port Huron for 10 years. The city keeps his memory alive with the Thomas Edison Depot Museum and Park.

Important Dates in Thomas Edison's Life

1847	Born on February 11 in Milan, Ohio
1854	Moves with his family to Port Huron, Michigan
1863	Begins working as a telegraph operator
1868	Applies for his first patent
1869	Moves to New York City and patents several telegraph devices
1870	Moves to Newark, New Jersey
1871	Marries Mary Stillwell on December 25
1876	Moves to Menlo Park, New Jersey, and builds a laboratory there
1877	Introduces the phonograph
1879	Invents the electric lightbulb
1881	Works on building electric power plants throughout the country
1884	Mary Edison dies
1886	Marries Mina Miller on February 24
1887	Moves into a larger laboratory in West Orange, New Jersey
1931	Dies on October 18 in Llewellyn Park, New Jersey

Glossary

charity—a group that helps people who are in need

fixtures—items that are permanently attached to something else

generators—machines that produce electricity

patent—a legal document that gives an inventor the right to make and produce an item; it prevents other people from stealing the idea

power plant—a building with equipment that produces electricity

stock tickers—machines that keep track of the current prices of companies' stocks

telegraph—a system that uses wires and codes to send messages over long distances

transmitter—a machine that sends out signals for communication devices

Did You Know?

- Thomas Edison's son Charles served as secretary of the Navy in 1940. He was also governor of New Jersey from 1941 to 1944.

- Henry Ford, the founder of Ford Motor Company, reconstructed the Menlo Park buildings in Dearborn, Michigan. They are completely restored and host thousands of visitors each year.

- Yankee Stadium in New York City was one of the buildings constructed with Edison's cement.

- Edison was presented with the Congressional Medal of Honor in 1928.

Want to Know More?

At the Library

Ford, Carin T. *Thomas Edison: Inventor.* Berkeley Heights, N.J.: Enslow Publishers, 2002.

Linder, Greg. *Thomas Edison.* Mankato, Minn.: Bridgestone Books, 1999.

Middleton, Haydn. *Thomas Edison: The Wizard Inventor.* New York: Oxford University Press, 1997.

On the Web

For more information on *Thomas Edison,* use FactHound to track down Web sites related to this book.

1. Go to *www.compasspointbooks.com/facthound*
2. Type in this book ID: 0756505674
3. Click on the *Fetch It* button.

Your trusty FactHound will fetch the best Web sites for you!

Through the Mail

Edison National Historic Site

Main Street and Lakeside Avenue

West Orange, NJ 07052

To learn more about Edison's work and his laboratory

On the Road

Edison Birthplace Museum

9 Edison Drive

Milan, OH 44846

To visit Edison's first home

Henry Ford Museum and Greenfield Village

20900 Oakwood Blvd.

Dearborn, MI 48124

To tour the restored Menlo Park laboratory

Index

About the Author

Lucia Raatma received her bachelor's degree in English literature from the University of South Carolina and her master's degree in cinema studies from New York University. She has written a wide range of books for young people. When she is not researching or writing, she enjoys going to movies, practicing yoga, and spending time with her husband, daughter, and golden retriever. She lives in New York.